WISDOM

D. Mehra & N.D. Mehra

southbank
publishing

First published in 2007 by Southbank Publishing
21 Great Ormond Street, London WC1N 3JB
In association with Rupa & Co, Delhi, India

www.southbankpublishing.com

A CIP catalogue record for this book is available from the British
Library.

ISBN 10: 1-904915-27-2

EAN 13: 978-1-904915-27-0

2 4 6 8 10 9 7 5 3 1

Typeset and designed by Alan Forster

Printed and bound in Great Britain by J.H.Haynes, Sparkford, Somerset

In memory of
D. Mehra and N.D. Mehra:

D. Mehra   1910 - 1997

N.D. Mehra   1924 - 1992

CONTENTS

※

Part II

※

Part III

Introduction

I first visited India in 1988 whilst working for Pan Books in the UK. Our distributor was Rupa & Co. When I first worked with R.K. Mehra, I had the pleasure of meeting D. Mehra and N.D. Mehra during my numerous visits to this great country.

On one occasion D. Mehra presented me with his book, *Other Men's Flowers* – a book of quotations for random reading. D. Mehra told me how he had pulled out the lines, phrases and paragraphs that appealed to him over a period of fifty years. The omission of authors' names was made for the sake of uniformity, as locating them was not possible in many cases. These gems make up Part II of this book.

D. Mehra was a great man and was born in Calcutta in 1910. He started a hosiery business under the name of Rupa & Co., and turned to the book trade at the inspiration of K. Jackson Marshall of William Collins Publishers, London. Rupa entered the world of publishing in 1960, the year of my birth.

N.D. Mehra was born on 13 October 1924 in Banaras. He worked with his uncle, D. Mehra, the founder of Rupa & Co in Calcutta. N.D. Mehra also read widely and, whilst studying the great religions and philosophers, gathered a unique collection of enduring observations. These were brought together in *Springs of Wisdom*, published by Rupa in 1993, one year after his death.

I'm very grateful to R.K. Mehra and his son Kapish Mehra for granting me permission to bring both books together as *Wisdom*.

Paul Torjussen
Southbank Publishing
August 2007

Part 1

African Wisdom

A bitter heart devours its owner.

— Herero wisdom

It is the rainy season that gives wealth.

— Hausa wisdom

When somebody says,
"The dead are happier than I am", let him
remember that his time will come.

— Baya wisdom

One does not have to learn how to fall into
a pit; all it takes is the first step, the others
take care of themselves.

— Wolof wisdom

It is better to know your own faults than those
of your neighbour.

– Serer wisdom

Much silence has a mighty noise.

– Swahili proverb

Three things are important in this world:
good health, peace with one's neighbour
and friendship with all.

– Serer wisdom

A man who suffers much knows much;
every day brings him new wisdom.

– Ewe wisdom

To know nothing is bad,
to learn nothing is worse.

– Serer wisdom

The rain does not fall on one roof.

– Ewe wisdom

God gives blessings to all men. If man had to distribute them, many would go without.

– Hausa wisdom

Follow three times the advice of a friend, but beware the advice of three friends.

– Wolof wisdom

A weak person goes where he is smiled at.

– Herero wisdom

Chinese Wisdom

A great man is one who
has not lost his child-like heart.

– Mencius

The contented man, even though poor, is happy;
the discontented man, even though rich, is sad.

– Anon

Greed makes man poor in this life,
for the abundance of this world does not make
him rich. Happy is he who is without sickness
and rich who is without debt.

– Anon

He that piles up treasure has much to lose.

– Lao-Tse

When something has happened, do not talk
about it; it is hard to collect spilled water.

– Anon

As long as you cannot forgive the next man
for being different, you are still far from the
path of wisdom.

– Anon

I have three treasures that I guard and cherish:
the first is love; the second is contentment; the
third is humility. Only the loving are courageous;
only the contented are magnanimous; only
the humble are capable of command.

– Lao-Tse

Do not fear going forward slowly; fear only
to stand still.

– Anon

Demand much of yourself and expect little of others. Thus you will be spared much vexation.

– Confucius

If I were to choose one sentence to sum up my whole philosophy, I should say: Allow no evil in your thoughts.

– Confucius

The noble man will only ask of his fellow-men what he expects of himself. He will fault in others only what he himself feels free of.

– Dseng-Dse

To have enough is happiness; to have more than enough is harmful. That is true of all things, but especially of money.

– Lao-Tse

Rather light a candle than
complain about darkness.

– Anon

Grant yourself a moment of peace
and you will understand how foolishly you
have scurried about. Learn to be silent and you
will notice that you have talked too much. Be
kind and you will realise that your judgement
of others was too severe.

– Tschen Tschi Ju

Greek Wisdom

Everywhere man blames nature and fate, yet his fate is mostly but the echo of his character and passions, his mistakes and weaknesses.

– Democritus

Happiness resides not in possessions and not in gold; the feeling of happiness dwells in the soul.

– Democritus

Men are not worried by things, but their ideas about things. When we meet with difficulties, become anxious or troubled, let us not blame others but rather ourselves, that is, our ideas about things.

– Epictetus

He only lives, who living enjoys life.

– Meander

Live today; forget the cares of the past.

– Epicurus

Remember, no human condition is ever permanent; then you will not be overjoyed in good fortune, nor too sorrowful in misfortune.

– Isocrates

One must not tie a ship to a single anchor, nor life to a single hope.

– Epictetus

Remember that you are only an actor in a play, which the manager directs.

– Epictetus

Happiness is self-contentedness.

– Aristotle

One is rich not through one's possessions, but through that which one can with dignity do without.

– Epicurus

If man is moderate and contented, then even age is no burden; if he is not, then even youth is full of cares.

– Plato

It is not good for all your wishes to be fulfilled: through sickness you recognise the value of health, through evil the value of good, through hunger satisfaction, through exertion the value of rest.

– Heraclitus

Bear patiently, my heart – for you have suffered
heavier things.

– Homer

A pleasant and happy life does not come from
external things; man draws within himself, as
from a spring, pleasure and joy.

– Plutarch

If you have a wounded heart, touch it as little
as you would an injured eye; there are only two
remedies for the suffering of the soul:
hope and patience.

– Pythagoras

He who submits to fate without complaint
is wise.

– Euripides

Danger can never be overcome without danger.

– Greek wisdom

Every man will fall who, though born a man,
proudly presumes to be superman.

– Sophocles

Look death in the face with joyful hope and
consider this a lasting truth: The righteous man
has nothing to fear, neither in life nor in death,
and the gods will not forsake him.

– Socrates

Indian Wisdom

What we have done will not be lost to all
eternity. Everything ripens at its time and
becomes fruit at its hour.

– Divyavadana

Only the ignorant man becomes angry. The
wise man understands.

– Indian wisdom

A thousand reasons for worry, a thousand
reasons for anxiety oppress day after day the
fool, but not the wise man.

– Hitopadesa of Narayana

A pure and strong will is all-powerful.

– Swami Vivekananda

Enjoy the pleasure bestowed on you
and bear the pain bestowed on you; wait
patiently for what time brings, as does
the farmer with the fruit.

– Mahabharata

Who is blind? – The man who cannot see
another world. Who is dumb? – The man who
cannot say a kind word at the right time.
Who is poor? – The man plagued with too
strong desires. Who is rich? – The man
whose heart is contented.

– Anon

The miser's money, which causes uneasiness,
hardship, blindness and sleeplessness, is not
money but a disease of the heart. Greed is not
stilled with money, any more than is
thirst with salt water.

– Ksemendra

Out of unreality lead us into reality.
Out of darkness lead us into light. From death
lead us into immortality.

– Upanishad

Let us overcome the angry man with
gentleness, the evil man with goodness, the
miser with generosity, the liar with truth.

– Mahabharata

The positive always defeats the negative:
courage overcomes fear, patience overcomes
anger and irritability, love overcomes hatred.

– Swami Vivekananda

The sun and moon are not mirrored in cloudy
waters, thus the Almighty cannot be mirrored
in a heart that is obsessed by the idea
of me and mine.

– Sri Ramakrishna

A small minded man weighs what can hinder
him and, fearful, dares not to set to work.
Difficulties cause the average man to leave off
what he has begun. A truly great man does not
slacken in carrying out what he has begun,
although obstacles tower thousand fold
until he has succeeded.

– Anon

Luck may sometimes help; work will always
help. If you do not worry about misfortune for
three years, it will become a blessing.

– The Brahmans

The smile that you send out returns to you.

– Anon

Islamic Wisdom

If you are content you are a king already.

– Ali's Hundred Sayings

Happiness comes to those who trust in it.

– Ali ibn Abi Talib

Two sorts of people will never have enough:
those who thirst for knowledge and those who
lust after riches.

– Arab saying

Life maybe short but a smile takes only
a second.

– Arab saying

Love is an incurable disease. No one who
catches it wants to recover and all its victims
refuse a cure.

– Ibn Hazm

There are ten commandments for the wise.
Nine say: 'Be silent!' One says: 'Say little!'

– Islamic saying

Lord, grant me firm intentions, unwavering
resolutions, a devoted heart and sincere words.
Lord, I ask only for what is good.

– Muhammad

Cover up your brother's or sister's weakness
and on the day of judgment God will forget
about your imperfection.

– Muhammad

We deceive ourselves our whole life long.
No hand can unravel the carpet of destiny, yet
no one is lost as long as he holds to God, the
beginning of every skein and every thread.

– Nisami

If you know your limits and find happiness in
observing them you can last a lifetime. But if
the false light of desire draws you ever
onwards, from one thing to another, you will
end in nothingness.

– Nisami

Forget your worries and leave everything to
destiny. Rejoice in the good fortune that smiles
on you now and forget your yesterdays.

– The 1001 Nights

Love and hatred are blinkers. With one you see
only good; with the other, bad.

– Turkish proverb

Remember that all suffering is followed by
joy and misfortune never comes unattended by
happiness.

– The 1001 Nights

Let fate run its course. Sleep the sleep
of the untroubled for in the very moment of
your anxiety the Almighty has changed
the face of things.

– The 1001 Nights

Hope without work is a tree without fruit.

– Arabic wisdom

Believe what you see and lay aside what you hear.

– Arabic wisdom

Eye of praise, eye of envy.

– Tunisian wisdom

The greatest luxury is simplicity.

– Kurdish wisdom

Fight for honour, for dishonour is easily won.

– Arabic wisdom

God is not seen; he is recognised by the mind.

– Arabic wisdom

Humility is the crown of manhood.

– Medieval Arabic wisdom

The ignorant man is a soldier without weapons.

– Arabic wisdom

The key to paradise is patience.

– Turkish wisdom

Even a moment's peace of mind surpasses
everything else you might strive after.

– Persian wisdom

Never sit where someone can tell you to move.

– Arabic wisdom

Listening requires more intelligence
than speaking.

– Turkish wisdom

Work is prayer.

– Arabic wisdom

Japanese Wisdom

No road is long with a friend at your side.

Darkness reigns at the foot of the lighthouse.

Joy and sorrow are life's companions.

After three years even a disaster can prove a blessing.

This day the moon's in the full, the next on the wane . . . the way of the world.

Not to lose patience when all patience seems gone . . . patience indeed.

Joy and suffering never leave us. Life is a long march with a heavy burden.

Even the thousand mile road has a first step.

Fortune comes to those who smile.

Jewish Wisdom

Condemn no man and consider nothing
impossible, for there is no man who does not
have a future and there is nothing that does
not have its hour.

– The Talmud

I grew up among wise men and found that there
is nothing better for man than silence.
Knowledge is not the main thing but deeds.

– Sayings of the Fathers

A miserly man is like a fattened ox;
he will give of his fat only when he has been
deprived of his life.

– Jewish proverb

Do not condemn your neighbour: You do not
know what you would have done in his place.

– Sayings of the Fathers

He who runs after good fortune runs
away from peace.

– Jewish proverb

He who wants to live his life should equip
himself with a heart which can stand suffering.
Man must realise that life is sometimes good
and sometimes bad. Only he is worthy of
respect who is grateful for the good and
knows how to bear evil.

– Jewish proverb

The heart of man and the bottom of the sea
are unfathomable.

– Jewish proverb

Man's great guilt does not lie in the sins that
he commits, for temptation is great and his
strength limited. Man's great guilt lies in the
fact that he can turn away from evil at any
moment and yet he does not.

– Rabbi Bunam

Men fall only in order to rise.

– Book of Zohar

The Kural

Be born if you must for fame or else
Better not be born at all.

The great do the impossible;
The mean cannot do it.

All other sins may be redeemed, but never in
gratitude.

Love is sweeter than wine – its mere thought
intoxicates.

When one likes pleasant words oneself, how
can one use harsh words to others?

Help given regardless of return
Is wider than the sea.

Does an envious man need enemies?

Envy, greed, wrath and harsh words ?
These four avoided is virtue.

The wealth which never declines
Is not riches but learning.

Wisdom is a weapon of defence,
An inner fortress no foe can quell.

The secret of success is humility;
It is also wisdom's weapon against foes.

It is base to be discourteous
Even to one's enemies.

Poverty is not a sin; it is a curse.

This world is dark even at noon
To those who cannot laugh.

Oriental Wisdom

Rejoice at your life, for the time is more
advanced than you think.

– Anon

Man has three ways of acting wisely: Firstly,
on meditation ? this is the noblest; secondly, on
imitation ? this is the easiest; and thirdly on
experience ? this is the bitterest.

– Confucius

Man cannot for a thousand days enjoy the
good, just as the flower cannot bloom
a hundred days.

– Tseng-Kuang

When you see a worthy person, endeavour to emulate him; when you see an unworthy person, then examine your inner self.

– Confucius

He who is really kind can never be unhappy; he who is really wise can never be confused; he who is really brave is never afraid.

– Confucius

Freedom from desire leads to inward peace.

– Lao-Tse

He who smiles rather than rages is always stronger.

– Japanese saying

The greatest revelation is stillness.

– Lao-Tse

One joy dispels a hundred cares.

– Anon

One moment of patience may ward off great disaster; one moment of impatience may ruin a whole life.

– Anon

He who understands others is learned. He who knows himself is wise. He who subdues himself is strong. He who is content is wealthy. He who does not lose his soul will endure.

– Lao-Tse

Kindness in words creates confidence; kindness in thinking creates profoundness; kindness in giving creates love.

– Lao-Tse

Persian Wisdom

Through love all things become lighter which
understanding thought too heavy.

– Hatif

Such are the ways of fate in this harsh world;
today you are lifted gently into the saddle and
tomorrow the saddle is placed on your
shoulders.

– Firdausi

Do not condemn your neighbour out of hand.
Be generous. Forgive. Pardon. Think of your
own failings. If each knew everything about the
other, he would forgive gladly and easily; there
would be no more pride, no more arrogance!

– Hafiz

If a word burns on your tongue, let it burn.

– Anon

Do you know what can never be satisfied?
The eye of greed: All the world's goods cannot
fill the abyss of its desire.

– Anon

The best thing that you can bring back from
your travels is yourself unscathed.

– Anon

He is nearest to self-knowledge and
self-realisation who accepts his lot contentedly,
for contentment is man's happiness, even in
the bitterness of daily life.

– Zun Hun

Roman Wisdom

It is a general human weakness to allow things,
uncertain and unknown, to set us up in hope,
or plunge us into fear.

– Gaius Caesar

There is nothing more painful than the insult
of human dignity, nothing more humiliating
than servitude. Human dignity and freedom
are our birthright. Let us defend them
or die with dignity.

– Cicero

Do not forget: A man needs little to lead
a happy life.

– Marcus Aurelius

Do not expect strangers to do for you what you
can do for yourself.

– Quintus Ennius

No sooner said than done, so acts your man
of worth.

– Quintus Ennius

When danger encircles you, show yourself
steadfast and undaunted; but when the winds
are too favourable, fail not to show wise caution
and haul in the billowing sail.

– Horace

Accept the things to which fate binds you and
love the people with whom fate brings you
together, but do so with all your heart.

– Marcus Aurelius

What a small portion of infinite and
immeasurable time is allotted to each of us. It
is so quickly swallowed up by eternity. How
small is the clod of earth on which you crawl
about. Remember all these things and consider
nothing great but this: Do what nature bids
you and suffer what life brings.

– Marcus Aurelius

Everywhere chance reigns; just cast out your
line and where you least expect it, there waits a
fish in the swirling waters.

– Ovid

Nothing is too hard for him who loves.

– Cicero

An easy task becomes difficult when you do it
with reluctance.

– Terence

Not he who has little, but he who desires
much is poor.

– Seneca

Money has never yet made anyone rich.

– Seneca

The miser does no one any good, but he treats
himself worst of all.

– Publilius Syrus

Russian Wisdom

Love is stronger than death and more powerful
than all fear of dying. Life lives only
through love.

– Îvan Turgenev

God is found in truth, not power.

– Alexander Nevsky

Indifference is a disease of the spirit.
It is premature death.

– Anton Chekov

We are human only because we love others
or have the opportunity to do so.

– Boris Pasternak

The meaning of human life is the
establishment of the kingdom of God on earth.
And that means the replacement of the egotistical,
hating, dictatorial and irrational things with a life
of brotherhood, freedom and reason.

– Leo Tolstoy

Day fades away with night and man with sorrow.

– Russian saying

The Lord who fills us with wisdom is great
indeed. But how does he do it? By means of
that very need we try to escape from. In care
and suffering he offers us experience
no book could ever hold.

– Nikolai Gogol

Repay evil with good and you deprive the
evildoer of all the pleasure of his wickedness.

– Leo Tolstoy

Part II

Anger is a short madness.

A faithful friend is the medicine of life.

A conference is a gathering of important
people who singly can do nothing, but together
can decide that nothing can be done.

A good meal shared with others is one of the
great joys of life.

A wise man puts aside ten per cent of the
money he gets, and ninety per cent of
the free advice.

A politician thinks of the next election;
a statesman, of the next generation.

A man never reveals his character more vividly
than when portraying the character of another.

Advice is something the wise don't need and
fools won't take.

Anger is never without reason, but seldom
a good one.

Anger is the end of reason and beginning
of calamity. Anger starts with foolishness and
ends with repentance.

A room without books is a body without a soul.

A happy couple: the husband deaf,
the wife blind.

A flatterer is a secret enemy.

A mob has many heads but no brain.

A partnership with the powerful is never safe.

All things are easy that are done willingly.

A truth that is told with bad intent beats all
the lies that you can invent.

Always laugh with others, never at them.

Accept the inevitable and don't dwell upon it.

All true happiness is an inner experience.

A good heart is better than a good mind.

A customer is the most important visitor on our premises. He is not dependent on us. We are dependent on him. He is not an interruption on our work. He is the purpose for it. He is not an outsider on our business. He is part of it. We are part of it. We are not doing him a favour by serving him. He is doing us a favour by giving us an opportunity to do so.

All is perishable in the world: Power and self will disappear, but the virtue of a great name will live forever.

B

Believe not all you hear and tell not
all you believe.

Be slow in choosing a friend, slower in
changing.

Betrayers are hated even by those whom
they benefit.

Blessed is the man who expects nothing, for he
shall never be disappointed.

Be an ambassador of good will to all people.

Business is not merely a matter of attending for a few hours, but it is a matter of thinking, dreaming, imagining and working. Industrial enterprise is in the long run not just a source of livelihood to the entrepreneur, but ought to be a way of life for him.

Beauty minus goodness = 0

Beauty is eternity gazing at itself in the mirror.

Belief consists of accepting the affirmations of the soul; unbelief, in denying them.

Believe those who are seeking the truth; doubt those who find it.

C

Critics are the men who have failed
in literature and art.

Count not too much on time to come.

Common sense is the most widely shared
commodity in the world, for every man is
convinced that he is well supplied with it.

Corruption begins at the top and seeps down.

Civilisation depends not only on human
creativeness but on the moral qualities
of gentleness and compassion.

Calm deliberation unravels every knot.

Character is like a tree and reputation like its shadow. The shadow is what we think of it; the tree is the real thing.

Character develops itself in the stream of life.

Childhood: The period of human life intermediate between the idiocy of infancy and the folly of youth – two removed from the sin of manhood and three from the remorse of age.

D

Death is the end of all woes.

Do all the good you can by all the means
you can in all the places you can at all the times
you can to all the people you can for as long
as ever you can.

Don't open a shop unless you like to smile.

Do as well as you can do today and perhaps
tomorrow you may be able to do better.

Diplomacy is to do and say the nastiest thing
in the nicest way.

Diplomat:
When he says "yes" he means "maybe". When
he says "maybe" he means "no". If he says
"no", he is not a diplomat.

Dignity is the opposite of humiliation.

Denial of God we have known, but denial of
truth, we have not known.

Democracy is the recurrent suspicion
that more than half of the people are right
more than half of the time.

E

Every excess becomes a vice.

Every light has its shadow.

Experience is the name we give to our mistakes.

Education is the transmission of civilisation.

Education: a debt due from present to future
generations.

Envy no one.

F

Friends come and go but enemies accumulate.

Fame leaves by the same door that conceit enters.

Flattery corrupts both the receiver and the giver.

Few friendships would survive if each one knew
what his friend says of him behind his back.

Failure is a man who has blundered but is not
capable of cashing in on the experience.

Freedom doesn't mean that you can do what
you please.

G

Gossiping and lying go together.

Great enterprise, boundless courage, tremendous energy and above all, perfect obedience – these are the only traits that lead to individual and national regeneration.

Give everyone the benefit of the doubt.

Great ideas often receive violent opposition from mediocre minds.

Greed is a fat demon with a small mouth and whatever you feed it is never enough.

Gratitude is not only the greatest of virtues
but the parent of all the others.

Good people do not need laws to tell them to
act responsibly, while bad people will find a
way around the laws.

Grief is itself a medicine.

He will never have true friends who is afraid
of making enemies.

He is not laughed at that laughs at
himself first.

Hold out a hand instead of pointing a finger.

Humility is a virtue.

He who will not reason is a bigot; he who
cannot is a fool; and he who dares not is
a slave.

Happiness depends on what you can give, not on what you can get.

He who receives a good turn should never forget it; he who does one should never remember it.

Happiness doesn't come from doing what we like to do but from liking what we have to do.

He who waits to do a great deal of good at once will never do anything.

Haste in judgement is criminal.

Happiness is an inner state of mind. It is little dependent on outside environment.

1

I cannot give you the formula for success, but I can give you the formula for failure – which is: Try to please everybody.

If your lips would keep from slips, five things observe with care; to whom you speak, of whom you speak and how and when and where.

In all things, success depends on previous preparation and without such preparation there is sure to be failure.

If a thing is right, never believe it to be impossible. Believe that it can be done and it will be done.

I disagree with what you say, but I will defend
to the death your right to say it.

If you want business you want a broad mind, a
genial smile, a cheery voice, a firm faith, an
undaunted spirit, a good hope, a brave heart
and untiring energy.

It is not tears but determination that
makes pain bearable.

I enjoy flattery and I do not think it does
you much harm unless you inhale.

It is a good thing to learn caution by the
misfortune of others.

Idle young man becomes unhappy old man.

Idealism and realism are not independent of
each other but are interdependent.

If you wish to be regarded as strange, erratic and peculiar, just tell the truth. There is scarcely any competition in this line.

It is injustice that breeds hatred.

Ideals are something we should like to reap in others, but fail to sow in ourselves. I listen from within: That time is a great healer of hurts, sorrows and disappointments. When one door closes another will open if we don't lose heart.

In order to receive, one must first learn to give.

It's better to be embarrassed than ashamed.

Indignation is a state of mind in which niceties of diplomatic calculation cannot possibly flourish.

If parents want honest children they should be honest themselves.

It is better to die on your feet then live on your knees.

In a conflict between the heart and the head I have always tried to follow the heart.

In the game of life older people become spectators instead of players.

Inspire others to live great lives.

If a child lives with ridicule, he learns to be shy. If a child lives with shame, he learns to feel guilty. If a child lives with tolerance, he learns to be patient. If a child lives with security, he learns to have faith.

I have never seen a man lost who was on a straight path.

J

Justice without wisdom is impossible.

Joy and sorrow are separable . . . together they
come and when one sits alone with you
remember that the other is asleep on your bed.

Justice is conscience, not a personal conscience
but the conscience of the whole of humanity.
Those who clearly recognise the voice of their
own conscience usually recognise also
the voice of justice.

Justice without force is powerless; force without
justice is tyrannical.

Judge people by the best, not by their best and not by their worst.

Judge others by their questions rather than by their answers.

K

Keep your fears to yourself but share your courage with others.

Kind words do not cost much, yet accomplish much.

Kindness has converted more sinners than zeal, eloquence or learning.

Kind words can be short and easy to speak but their echoes are truly endless.

Kindness is more important than wisdom and the recognition of this is the beginning of wisdom.

Knowing is not enough; we must apply.

L

Liars ought to have good memories.

Life hangs by an uncertain thread.

Love your enemy for they tell your faults.

Learn to listen, then listen to learn.

Little harm will come of being stupid, until the fellow thinks himself clever. Pretended wisdom is the worst of stupidity.

Love comes unseen – we only see it go.

Laughter is the best medicine for a long
and happy life.

Law must be based on justice not power.

Leaders shouldn't attach moral significance
to their ideas: Do that and you
can't compromise.

Men are seldom in the right when they guess
at a woman's mind.

Mistakes are often the best teachers.

Man cannot buy time.

My rule was always to do the business of the
day in the day.

Many a man looking for sympathy really needs
two swift kicks properly placed.

Man is an egoist par excellence.
He parades his virtues, palliates his faults,
magnifies his misfortunes and sets up his own
arbitrary standard of right and wrong whereby
he measures humanity and judges the world.

Mothers need no monuments of granite to
commemorate them, for they live for ever in
almost everyone's heart.

Men have sight, women have insight.

Marriage is the triumph of imagination over
intelligence.

Marriage is the triumph of hope over
experience.

Ninety per cent of inspiration is perspiration.

Never answer a question until asked.

No one can get through life without failures and mistakes. Admit your mistake; regret it; learn from it.

Never maintain an argument with heat and clamour, though you think or know yourself to be in the right.

No one is as deaf as the man who will not listen.

No gift is more precious than good advice.

No God, no peace – know God, know peace.

No one needs help to get into trouble.

No garments can conceal character. The man comes out sooner or later.

Nothing will give you greater peace than the patient bearing of insult.

Next to education, practical experience is the best thing.

Nature, time and patience are the three great physicians.

Old men go to death, but death comes to
young men.

Observation, not old age, brings wisdom.

Open rebuke is better than secret hatred.

Our greatest glory is not in never falling but
in rising every time we fall.

Only a life lived for others is
a life worthwhile.

One photograph is worth a thousand words.

Opinions ought to be weighed; they ought not be counted. Majority is no proof of truth.

Our wisdom comes from our experiences and our experience comes from our foolishness.

One must not grieve excessively over the one who is gone to the Great Beyond, for the departed one lives in spirit forever.

P

Poor men want meat for their stomachs;
rich men, stomachs for their meat.

Progress is impossible without change, and
those who cannot change their minds cannot
change anything.

Patience is the best remedy for every trouble.

People who know little are usually great talkers,
while men who know much say little.

Punctuality is the soul of the business.

Perfection consists not in doing extraordinary things but in doing ordinary things extraordinary well.

Promotion is only an art when you sell something nobody wants.

Privilege creates responsibility.

Pride must be balanced with humility.

R

Rare is the union of beauty and modesty.

Rumour is a great traveller.

Reading is to the mind what exercise is
to the body.

Remember that today is really the tomorrow of
which you expected so much yesterday.

Reading makes better citizens and happier
individuals. It is also the means of preserving
and sustaining the solid foundations
of culture and learning.

Reality is merely an illusion, albeit a very persistent one.

Reality does not conform to the ideal.

Readers are plentiful; thinkers are rare.

S

Sleep is better than medicine.

Success has brought many to destruction.

Self-trust is the first secret to success.

Shallow men believe in luck; strong men believe
in cause and effect.

Success is most enjoyable when it has been
won against the odds.

Speed has five letters. So has death.

Self-justification is worse than the original offence.

Selfishness is a sin whether in individuals or nations.

Success consists of going from failure to failure without loss of enthusiasm.

Spiritual paralysis is death in life.

T

Though old and wise, one still needs advice.

The best way to teach character is to have it
around the house.

The easiest way to get money is to earn it.

The test of courage is to bear defeat,
without losing heart.

The easiest way to dignity is humility.

Truth needs no memory.

To know how to grow old is the master work of
wisdom and one of the most difficult chapters
in the great art of living.

There is no substitute for good parents.

The diseases of old age are not due to old age,
they are due to wrong life.

The pleasures of the senses pass quickly. Those
of the heart become sorrows. But those of the
mind are with us even to the end of our journey.

Take no bribe. Surrender no right.

The rich have heirs not children.

The secret of success lies not in
doing your own work, but in recognising the
right person to do it.

The only person never to make a mistake was the man who never did anything.

To succeed, we must first believe that we can.

The foundation of every noble character is absolute sincerity.

The more luxuriously you live, the more exercise you require.

Tycoons climb to the top of the tree and find nothing there.

Time heals sorrow.

What is easy is seldom excellent.

Write injuries in sand, benefits in marble.

Words should be weighed not counted.

When a man's head is empty some nonsense
or other is sure to get in.

With only fifteen minutes a day you can read
twenty books a year.

Wise men change their minds, fools never.

Courtesy

Courtesy costs nothing and brings the highest
dividends in the game of life.

Courtesy improves memory.

Courtesy builds character – expressed in the
ego, soul and personality.

Courtesy develops observation and comparison.

Courtesy wins friends and educates them.

Courtesy develops self-control.

Courtesy develops diplomacy.

Courtesy develops humility.

Courtesy develops consideration for others.

Courtesy develops a finer sense of spiritual values.

It's not always easy…

To apologise

To begin over

To admit error

To be unselfish

To take advice

To be charitable

To keep trying

To think and then act

To be considerate

To profit by mistake

To forgive and forget

To shoulder deserved blame

But

It always pays.

A Good Rule

It is a good rule to hope for the best.

Never anticipate evils.

Learn never to conceive prejudice against others, because you know nothing of them.

Never despise anyone for anything he cannot help, least of all for his poverty.

Never despise anyone at all.

Be neither a martyr, nor sycophant.

True equality is the only true morality or true wisdom.

Believe all the good you can of everyone.

Envy none.

Never quarrel with tried friends or those you wish to continue as such.

Do not gratify the enemies of liberty by putting yourself at their mercy.

Avoid

Politics without principle

Wealth without work

Pleasure without conscience

Knowledge without character

Business without morality

Science without humanity

Worship without sacrifice

A letter should be ...

Respectful to superiors

Courteous to inferiors

Familiar to friends

Affectionate to relations

Simple to children

Tender and sympathetic in condolence

Lively and joyous in congratulations

Forcible and impressive in weighty matters

Easy and sprightly on lighter subjects

Very clear in commercial correspondence

Above all else, it must be sincere.

The spoken word

Nature knew her business when she gave us two ears and only one mouth.

Conversational interest is based upon making another feel important and replacing telling with asking.

The less we say the less we have to take back.

Settle disputes as quickly as possible. Every moment of delay adds coal to the fires of dissension.

The tongue being in a wet place is apt to slip when going very fast.

The Earthling

Countless years ago the people of Alzorus
used the planet Earth as a lunatic asylum.
They called the people they dumped there
'Earthlings'.
I am an earthling.
My memory goes back a long way.
I was dumped here long ago.
I lived beneath some overhanging rocks.
Around me at night, through the sky's
black sheet, stars poured down.
It was lonely sitting for centuries beneath that
rain-drenched rock, wrapped in furs, afraid of
this whole terrible planet.
I grew fed up with the taste of its food.
I made fire; I slaughtered creatures;
I walked through a forest and made friends.
I copied the things they made.
I walked through another forest and found
enemies.

I destroyed the things they made.
I went on and on and on and on
and on a bit more.
I crossed mountains; I crossed new oceans.
I became familiar with this world.
Time would not stop running when I asked it.
I could not whistle for it to come back.
I invented a couple of languages.
I wrote things down.
I invented books.
Time passed.
My inventions piled up.
The natives of this planet feared me.
Some tried to destroy me.
Rats came.
A great plague swept over the world.
Many of me died.
I am an earthling.
I invented cities. I tore them down.
I sat in comfort. I sat in poverty.
I sat in boredom.
Home was a planet called Alzorus.
A tiny far-off star –
One night it went out. It vanished.
I am an earthling, exiled for ever from my
beginnings.

Time passed. I did things. Time passed.
I grew exhausted.
One day a great fire swept the world.
I wanted to go back to the beginning.
It was impossible.
The rock I had squatted under melted.
Friends became dust,
Dust became the only friend.
In the dust I drew faces of people.
I am putting this message on a feather
and puffing it up among the stars.
I have missed so many things out!
But this is the basic story, the terrible story.
I am an earthling,
I was dumped here a long time ago.
Mistakes were made.

– Brian Patten

Part III

Advertising

Advertising agency: eighty five per cent confusion and fifteen per cent commission.

– Fred Allen

When business is good it pays to advertise; when business is bad you've got to advertise.

– Anon

An editor is one who separates the wheat from the chaff and prints the chaff.

– Adlai Stevenson

You can fool all of the people all of the time
if the advertising is right and the budget
is big enough.

– Joseph Levine

Advice after injury is like medicine after death.

– Proverb

Doing business without advertising is like
winking at a girl in the dark: You know what
you are doing but nobody else does.

– Edgar Watson Howe

Advertising is the very essence of democracy.

– Bruce Barton

Age

One of the many pleasures of old age is
giving things up.

– Malcolm Muggeridge

Young men think old men fools and old men
know young men to be so.

– Proverb

If you wish good advice consult an old person.

– Proverb

You can never plan the future by the past.

– Edmund Burke

It is always wise to look ahead, but difficult to look farther than you can see.

– Winston Leonard Spencer

Study the past if you would divine the future.

– Confucius

It is not enough to have a good mind: the main thing is to use it well.

– René Descartes

Business Wisdom

No nation was ever ruined by trade.

– Benjamin Franklin

One machine can do the work of fifty
ordinary men. No machine can do the work of
one extraordinary man.

– Elbert Hubbard

The selfish spirit of commerce knows no
country and feels no passion or principles but
that of gain.

– Thomas Jefferson

The best way to keep your word is not to give it.

– Napoléon Bonaparte

A merchant's happiness hangs upon chance, wind and waves.

– Edmond Fuller

Where wealth and freedom reign, contentment fails. And honour sinks where commerce long prevails.

– Oliver Goldsmith

The art of winning in business is in working hard – not taking things too seriously.

– Elbert Hubbard

Business is more exciting than any game.

– Lord Beaverbrook

Whenever you see a successful business,
someone once made a courageous decision.

– Peter F. Drucker

Punctuality is one of the cardinal business
virtues: Always insist on it in your
subordinates.

– Donald Robert Perry Marquis

If you wish to succeed in life, make
perseverance your bosom friend, experience your
wise counsellor, caution your elder brother and
hope your guardian genius.

– Joseph Addison

A man is to go about his business as if he had
not a friend in the world to help him at it.

– Lord Halifax

There are no gains without pains.

– Adlai Stevenson

Where money talks there are few interruptions.

– Herbert V. Prochnow

To open a shop is easy; to keep it open is an art.

– Confucius

Live together like brothers and do business like strangers.

– Arabic proverb

A page digested is better than a volume hurriedly read.

– Thomas Babington Macaulay

Business, you know, may bring you money, but friendship hardly ever does.

– Jane Austen

Live together like brothers and do business like strangers.

– Arabic proverb

A business must have a conscience as well as a counting house.

– Sir Montague Burton

What is a committee? A group of the unwilling, picked from the unfit, to do the necessary.

– Richard Harkness

Punctuality is the soul of business.

– Proverb

Comment is free but facts are sacred.

– C.P. Scott

What you get free costs too much.

– Jean Anouilh

First learn the meaning of what you say
and then speak.

– Epictetus

Genius is one per cent inspiration and
ninety-nine per cent perspiration.

– Thomas Alva Edison

Experience is the best teacher.

– Proverb

Men of few words are the best men.

– William Shakespeare

Second thoughts are even wiser.

– Euripides

All work and no play makes Jack a dull boy.

– Proverb

The ballot is stronger than the bullet.

– Abraham Lincoln

Live and learn.

– Proverb

Consolation

Inasmuch as love grows in you, so in you
beauty grows. For love is the beauty of the soul.

– St Augustine

Only one principle will give you courage;
that is the principle that no evil lasts for ever
nor indeed very long.

– Epicurus

Prosperity is not without many fears and
distastes and adversity is not without
comforts and hopes.

– Francis Bacon

One virtue stands out above all others: the
constant striving upwards, wrestling with
oneself, the unquenchable desire for greater
purity, wisdom, goodness and love.

– Goethe

One must have spiritual strength and
remain brave and cheerful in these hard times.
Pain and suffering are but externals; for such
things it is not worth losing God's love
and the ability to smile.

– Guy De Larigaudie

How ridiculous and unrealistic is the man who
is astonished at anything that happens in life.

– Marcus Aurelius

What fates impose, that men must needs abide.
It boots not to resist both wind and tide.

– William Shakespeare

Man can climb the highest summits, but he
cannot dwell there long.

– George Bernard Shaw

Enjoy life, employ life.
It flits away and will not stay.

– Proverb

Suffering is a misfortune, as viewed from
the one side and a discipline, as viewed from
the other.

– Samuel Smiles

Friendship

What is a friend?
– A single soul dwelling in two bodies.

– Aristotle

In love all of life's contradictions dissolve and
disappear. Only in love are unity and duality
not in conflict.

– Rabindranath Tagore

The holy passion of friendship is of so
sweet and steady and loyal enduring a nature
that it will last through a whole lifetime if not
asked to lend money.

– Mark Twain

I have lived long enough to know that the
evening glow of love has its own riches and
splendour.

– Benjamin Disraeli

Of all the gifts that a wise providence grants
us to make life full and happy, friendship is the
most beautiful.

– Epicurus

Experience teaches us that love does not
consist of two people looking at each other, but
of looking together in the same direction.

– Antoine de Saint-Exupéry

When one has once fully entered the realm of
love, the world – no matter how imperfect –
becomes rich and beautiful, for it consists solely
of opportunities for love.

– Kierkegaard

To love someone is to be the only one to see a miracle invisible to others.

– François Mauriac

Friendship is simply loving agreement in all life's questions.

– Cicero

One can do without people, but one has need of a friend.

– Chinese saying

A friend may well be reckoned the masterpiece of nature.

– Ralph Waldo Emerson

It is not a lack of love but a lack of friendship that makes unhappy marriages.

– Nietzsche

I know not, I ask not, if guilt's in thy heart, but
I know that I love thee, whatever thou art.

– Thomas Moore

If I should meet thee after long years, how
should I greet thee? With silence and tears.

– Lord Byron

Laughter is not at all a bad beginning for a
friendship and it is far the best ending for one.

– Oscar Wilde

Friendship is the shadow at evening;
it grows until the sun of life sets.

– Jean De La Fontaine

To love someone means to see him as God
intended him.

– Dostoevsky

Happiness
and laughter

No pleasure is comparable to standing upon
the vantage ground of truth.

– Francis Bacon

Happiness begins for us when we have put an
end to our pretensions for they bring us, after
all, nothing but pain and discomfort.

– Nicolas Chamfort

No one can forge a lifetime of happiness, only
ever the happiness of the moment.

– Waggerl

An hour of concentrated work does more to kindle joy, to overcome sadness and to set your ship afloat again than a month of gloomy brooding.

– Benjamin Franklin

The supreme happiness of life is the conviction that we are loved.

– Victor Hugo

The bible charges us to love our neighbours and our enemies; probably because they are usually the same people.

– Chesterton

Genuine joy grows not from contemplation, not from riches and not from fame, but from work that has its own inner value.

– Wilfred Grenfell

The most lost day of all is the day on which we
do not laugh.

– Nicolas Chamfort

To conquer a joy is more valuable than giving
oneself up to a sorrow.

– André Gide

The most important piece of luggage is and
remains a joyful heart.

– Hermann Löns

Miser and a fat pig will only be of use when dead.

– Logau

By swallowing evil words unsaid no one has
ever yet harmed his stomach.

– Winston Churchill

A jest, a laughing word, often decides the highest matters better than sharpness and seriousness.

– Horace

It is worthier of man to rise in laughter above life than to bewail it. He is more worthy of the human race who laughs at it, than he who sheds tears over it.

– Seneca

Men are not always what they seem but seldom better.

– Lessing

Serenity and joyfulness are the Sun under which everything thrives.

– Jean Paul

Only for the happy man does the tree of life flower.

– Ernst Moritz Arndt

What men commonly call their fate is mostly only their own foolishness.

– Schopenhauer

There are two tragedies in life: one is not to get your heart's desire; the other is to get it.

– George Bernard Shaw

What a piece of work is a man! says the poet. Yes: but what a blunderer!

– George Bernard Shaw

Ask God's blessing on your work but do not also ask him to do it.

– Waggerl

Hope

At the edge of despair dawns a clarity in which
one is almost happy.

– Jean Anouilh

Misfortune is an occasion to demonstrate
character.

– Seneca

Hopelessness is anticipated defeat.

– Karl Jaspers

What is a man finally left with? Hope.

– Diogenes

As long as hope remains only a coward will despair.

– Bertrand Russell

There is a law in life: When one door closes to
us another one opens.

– André Gide

We do not become free by refusing to
acknowledge something above us, but by
respecting something above us.

– Goethe

Deprive the average man of his life's illusions
and you rob him of his happiness.

– Ibsen

Should a single disappointed hope make us so
hostile towards the world?

– Lessing

Hope walks with life,
only in death does hope end.

– Theocritus

Hope is like the clouds:
some pass by; others bring rain.

– Abu al-Ala al-Maarri

That is the mystery of grace:
It never comes too late.

– Francois Mauriac

Love your calling with passion; it is the
meaning of your life.

– Auguste Rodin

Oh Wind,
If winter comes, can spring be far behind?

– Shelley

True hope is swift and flies
with swallow's wings;
Kings it makes gods
and meaner creatures kings.

– William Shakespeare

I slept and dreamed that life was joy;
I awoke and saw that life was duty, acted
and behold: Duty was joy.

– Tagore

If you have hoped and your expectation was
not fulfilled, then go on hoping.

– Talmund

We have no ultimate assurance,
we have only hope.

– Ernst Bloch

The most distant goal is attainable to him
who hopes wisely.

– Lope De Vega

The boldest and most ridiculous hope
has sometimes been the cause of extraordinary
success.

– Vauvenargues

Love

Love seeketh not itself to please
Nor for itself hath any care,
But for another gives its ease
And builds a heaven in hell's despair.

– William Blake

All who joy would win must share it –
happiness was born a twin.

– Byron

To be able to find joy in another's joy:
That is the secret of happiness.

– Georges Bernanos

What charms are there in the harmony of minds
and in a friendship founded on mutual esteem
and gratitude.

– David Hume

It is not the perfect but the imperfect who have
need of love.

– Oscar Wilde

Serenity is neither frivolity, nor complacency:
it is the highest knowledge and love; it is the
affirmation of all reality being awoke at the
edge of all deeps and abysses. Serenity is the
secret of beauty and the real substance
of all art.

– Hermann Hesse

Love sought is good, but given unsought
is better.

– William Shakespeare

Real love begins when nothing is expected
in return.

– Antoine de Saint-Exupéry

What a man is to himself, what accompanies
him into solitude and what no one can give him
or take away from him, this is evidently more
important to him than everything he may
possess or what he is in the eyes of others.

– Schopenhauer

We shall never plumb the depths and the
ultimate mysteries of life. The only thing that
really matters is what we make of our lives.

– Thornton Wilder

God has more love and mercy than man can
ever sin against.

– N. Lenau

Money

The two most beautiful words in the English language are 'Cheque Enclosed'.

– Dorothy Parker

Money has no legs, but it runs.

– Japanese proverb

Bad money drives out good money.

– Thomas Gresham

It is better to live rich than to die rich.

– Samuel Johnson

A man is usually more careful of his money
than he is of his principles.

– Edgar Watson Howe

Money, it turned out, was exactly like sex:
You thought of nothing else if you didn't have it
and thought of other things if you did.

– James Baldwin

A man without money is like a wolf
without teeth.

– Proverb

We ask not what he is but what he has.

– Proverb

Prosperity is a great teacher; adversity is greater.

– William Hazlitt

The prosperity of this world is like writing
on water.

– Hindu proverb

Nothing is more humiliating than to see
idiots succeed in enterprises we have failed in.

– Gustave Flaubert

Success and failure are both difficult to endure.
Along with success come drugs, divorce,
fornication, bullying, travel, meditation,
depression, neurosis and suicide.
With failure comes failure.

– Joseph Heller

The greatest thing in the world is to know
how to be self-sufficient.

– Michel de Montaigne

Success has ruined many a man.

– Benjamin Franklin

Success is that old ABC – ability, breaks and
courage.

– Charles Luckman

On the day of victory no fatigue is felt.

– Proverb

As wealth is power, so all power will infallibly
draw wealth to itself by some means or other.

– Edmond Burke

Man can climb to the highest summits,
but he can not dwell there long.

– George Bernard Shaw

There is no success without hardship.

– Sophocles

The first wealth is health

– Ralph Waldo Emerson

Success has many friends.

– Proverb

No just man ever becomes rich suddenly.

– Menander

When I was young I thought money was
the most important thing in life:
Now that I am old I know that it is.

– Oscar Wilde

Music

The musician's art is to send light into the
depths of men's hearts.

– Robert Schumann

Music is the only bodiless entry into a higher
world of knowledge which comprehends
mankind, but is not comprehended by it.

– Beethoven

For those who do not love music drives away
hate. Music gives peace to the restless and
comforts the sorrowful. They who no longer
know where to turn find new ways and those who
have despaired gain new confidence and love.

– Pablo Casals

All art constantly aspires towards the
condition of music.

– Walter Pater

Music must serve a purpose; it must be part of
something larger than itself, a part of humanity.

– Pablo Casals

Music is the meditation between the
intellectual and the sensuous life.

– Beethoven

Politics

Political skill is the ability to foretell what is going to happen tomorrow, next week, next month and next year. And to have the ability afterwards to explain why it didn't happen.

– Winston Churchill

Public money is like holy water; everyone helps himself.

– Italian proverb

Whenever you have an efficient government you have a dictatorship.

– Harry S. Truman

Politicians are the same all over. They promise to build a bridge even when there's no river.

– Nikita Khrushchev

He knows nothing and he thinks he knows everything. That points clearly to a political career.

– George Bernard Shaw

Politics, as the word is commonly understood, are nothing but corruptions.

– Jonathan Swift

Success

All decent people live beyond their incomes nowadays and those who aren't respectable live beyond other people's. A few gifted individuals manage to do both.

– Saki (Hector Hugo Munro)

A man who is always ready to believe what is told him will never do well, especially a businessman.

– Petronius Gaius

The best executive is the one who has the sense enough to pick good men to do what he wants done and self-restraint enough to keep from meddling with them while they do it.

– Theodore Roosevelt

If you aspire to the highest place, it is no disgrace to stop at the second or even third place.

– Cicero

He who climbs the ladder must begin at the bottom.

– Proverb

Failure makes people bitter and cruel. Success improves the character of a man.

– W. Somerset Maugham

To be successful, a woman has to be better at her job than a man.

– Golda Meir

Experience is the name everyone gives to their mistakes.

– Oscar Wilde

Failure teaches success.

– Proverb

I would prefer even to fail with honour
than win by cheating.

– Sophocles

Management is the art of getting other people
to do all the work.

– Anon

A bad workman always blames his tools.

– Proverb

If you want a thing done well, do it yourself.

– Napoléon

Travel

Travel teaches toleration.

– Benjamin Disraeli

A gentleman ought to travel abroad but dwell
at home.

– Thomas Fuller

He that travels much, knows much.

– Thomas Fuller

Travel broadens the mind.

– Proverb

A pleasant companion reduces the length of the journey.

– Publilius Syrus

He who would travel happily must travel light.

– Antoine de Saint-Exupéry

The more I see of other countries the more I love my own.

– Madame de Staël